THE RAISING OF LAZARUS
BY SEBASTIANO DEL PIOMBO

The Raising of Lazarus by Sebastiano Del Piombo

CECIL GOULD

The National Gallery
Printed for the Trustees
1967

Designed by Paul Sharp
Printed by Alabaster Passmore and Sons Ltd
London and Maidstone

List of Illustrations

Foreword

The immediate occasion of this publication might best be described as the unveiling of Sebastiano's picture, great in every sense and registered as No. 1 in the Collection but scarcely seen before in living memory. The extraneous film which covered it until recently contained bitumen and brown pigment, and was much darker and more opaque even than the later stages of the notorious 'gallery varnish' of the National Gallery's first twenty years. Since this giant canvas in brown monochrome was taken to Wales with the rest of the Collection in 1939, it has appeared for a short time in an exhibition room only because there was then nowhere else to put it, and the room was next to the temporary Conservation Studio from which it could be kept under observation. Its rescue seemed an almost hopeless task, and no mention was made of it in the first National Gallery *Report*, which records the setting up of the Conservation Department under the Chief Restorer in 1954 and describes some of the physical problems then to be faced. The problem was a total one, involving not only surface accretions but the entire structure of the picture, which had been transferred from a wooden support to canvas in the eighteenth century. This is not the place to describe the means by which since 1958 it has been slowly brought back to a secure existence and to something like its original appearance.

Elucidation of a kind complementary to the cleaning is the purpose of the text by Cecil Gould which follows. He has been able to go with more detail than was possible in his Catalogue of the Sixteenth-Century Venetian School of 1959 into the fascinating conundrum of the historic picture's origin and the degree of Michelangelo's partisan participation. Also there are seventeen illustrations.

We hope it may be only the first of such booklets. The mammoth tasks of the Keeper staff in producing the detailed Sectional Catalogue by schools and the illustration of the entire Collection by volumes of large plates designed to accompany the texts, and of the Publications Department in financing it, are now very nearly completed. At last there is a little time and much more money to branch out into something more intimate and, we hope, more entertaining. Every great picture has a history, and there is virtually no limit to the themes for further essays which the National Gallery has to offer.

Philip Hendy,
DIRECTOR
31 October, 1967

Fig 1 Narbonne; The Cathedral

Fig 2 Raphael *Cardinal Giulio de' Medici*
Detail from portrait of Pope Leo X and cardinals
Florence, Pitti Palace

8

The city of Narbonne, for which Sebastiano's *Raising of Lazarus* was painted and where it remained for about two centuries, lies in a plain, some 50 miles north of the Pyrenees and the Spanish frontier. The cathedral of St. Just, for which the picture was destined, remains unfinished to this day, but its huge Gothic choir has one of the highest vaults in France and is among the most spacious and impressive of any of them [Fig 1].

The beauties of its mediaeval architecture would probably have been lost on a 16th-century archbishop, and particularly a foreign one. But the question did not arise, since the Italian who was in fact nominated to the see in 1515 was unlikely to visit Narbonne and seems never to have done so. He was Cardinal Giulio de' Medici [Fig 2], a cousin of the Pope, Leo X. Later, in 1523, Giulio was himself to become Pope with the title of Clement VII. He was the son of that Giuliano de' Medici who had been assassinated in the Pazzi conspiracy of 1478, when Giuliano's brother, Lorenzo the Magnificent, had barely escaped with his life. Giulio was born in that same year. He was a posthumous child and, it was widely believed, also illegitimate. In consequence Leo X, who favoured him, had been at pains to concoct a document which stated that Giuliano had been secretly married to Giulio's mother.

In May 1513, only two months after he became Pope, Leo X had nominated his cousin archbishop of Florence, creating him a cardinal four months later. The additional appointment to Narbonne, two years later still, was probably inspired by a political motive, but it seems to have convinced Cardinal Giulio of the desirability of making some graceful gesture to the cathedral which he was unlikely to grace with his presence. And the result of this was the huge altarpiece which is now in the National Gallery.

Cardinal Giulio was living in Rome at the time, and might be expected to employ a local artist. There was no lack of them. Indeed, there might have seemed an embarrassing riches, as it so happened that Leonardo, Michelangelo and Raphael were all in Rome in the year 1515. Some reflection, however, would have convinced an informed person that among these giants the choice, for practical purposes, was not quite so great as it seemed. For Leonardo, in his 'sixties, was more undecided and dilatory than ever and was thought to be wasting his time making weird scientific experiments in the Vatican, while Michelangelo, having finished the Sistine ceiling, was desperately trying to finish the sculptures for the Julian tomb. It is possible that the Cardinal tried to persuade him to undertake the work; if so, Michelangelo would have refused to be involved directly.

That left Raphael, who was in fact commissioned for the job. Unfortunately we do not know precisely when this occurred, and this affects our understanding of the initial order of events which is obscure in several respects. For by January 1517, a second painter, Sebastiano del Piombo, was working in rivalry with Raphael for the same purpose. It is probable, though not certain, that Raphael had been called in before Sebastiano. The Cardinal presumably reasoned that as Raphael was being grossly overworked by the Pope he might delay indefinitely. The commissioning of a rival might therefore be expected to spur him, and if it did, he, the Cardinal, could take his choice from the two altarpieces. It was in this way that Michelangelo came, after all, to be indirectly involved.

For at this time there was rivalry between him and Raphael. How much of it was due to genuine friction between the principals and how much to the intrigues and lobbyings of their respective factions cannot be decided, and in any case the struggle may have been exaggerated by historians writing after the event. The most important of these, Giorgio Vasari, was indeed an avowed partisan of Michelangelo's, and though some of what he says is corroborated by surviving letters a great deal is not.

Moreover, Vasari's partisanship in this instance was rather more complicated than usual. It was not merely that he knew Michelangelo personally and worshipped him, and for that reason was biased against Raphael, whom he had never known. In addition to this he had known Sebastiano personally, and did not entirely approve of him. To the extent, therefore, that Raphael opposed Michelangelo he was out of Vasari's favour, but as long as Sebastiano followed Michelangelo's precepts he was in it.

The young Venetian, Sebastiano, afterwards called 'del Piombo' when he became Keeper of the Papal Seal, had been brought to Rome in 1511 by the Sienese banker, Agostino Chigi, and put to work in Chigi's villa, the Farnesina. Soon he had come under the influence, personal as well as artistic, of Michelangelo. According to what Vasari implies Michelangelo had been annoyed by the partisans of Raphael who had claimed that the latter was a better painter than he, Michelangelo. Michelangelo had only draughtsmanship to offer, Raphael all the other qualities of a painter. Vasari states that it was Michelangelo's own idea to use Sebastiano as a pawn in his struggle with Raphael, thinking that Sebastiano's skill, as a Venetian, as colourist, allied to skill in draughtsmanship which Michelangelo would supply for him, should result in paintings which would be more highly esteemed than Raphael's. If this account is entirely true it would mean that Michelangelo was more interested that *somebody* should surpass Raphael than in getting the credit for it himself, since Vasari expressly states that Michelangelo did not wish to be directly involved, but only 'under cover of a third party'.

We may question if the opposition of 'draughtsmanship' and 'colour', which had become something of a war-cry by the time Vasari wrote in the mid-16th century, was already a specific issue as early as this. If it was, the avowed object of the exercise, as stated by Vasari, would have been defeated to some extent, since Sebastiano, under the influence of Michelangelo and the Antique, was at this time striving to throw off his Venetian heritage as a colourist and to paint in the Roman manner. The recent (1967) cleaning of the *Raising of Lazarus*, which has revealed the colours for the first time within living memory, confirms this. The colours are not tonally related, as in Venetian painting, nor is the paint sensuously applied. Instead, Sebastiano uses evocative and strange colours in new combinations – orange of different shades combined with green of different shades, or a rare and beautiful eau-de-Nil (in the man behind Lazarus) combined with white.

The motives of Sebastiano in agreeing to work in these circumstances are curious and interesting. The idea of being used as a pawn in other people's quarrels would not appeal to every artist as genuinely gifted as he was. Perhaps his talent was of the kind, by no means unknown, which responds best to stimulus from another artist, making him, in the event, a natural collaborator. At all events he showed no opposition to the plan. On the contrary, he gave every indication of being inspired by the idea of painting from Michelangelo's designs – as, indeed, other painters such as Pontormo, Venusti and others were to do later in the century. Cardinal Giulio's altarpiece was not the only instance of the collaboration. Sebastiano had already drawn on Michelangelo's designs in an altarpiece for Viterbo and in a chapel in S. Pietro in Montorio in Rome. In these cases there had been no question of direct confrontation with Raphael, as in the Narbonne altarpiece, though Michelangelo may well have been animated by the same idea. And Cardinal Giulio, for his part, may well have heard of the Michelangelo-Sebastiano collaboration and considered it the next best thing to Michelangelo himself. By commissioning Sebastiano he would, in a sense, be getting Michelangelo as well.

As to Raphael, he was said not to relish the challenge, but on this our only information comes from the other side. On the 19th January 1517 Leonardo the Saddler, a friend of Michelangelo's who seems to have shared his house in Rome, wrote to him saying 'Sebastiano has received money to buy the wood [for the *Raising of Lazarus*] but I have the impression that Raphael is moving heaven and earth to stop him doing anything, so as not to have to stand the comparison' (it is this letter which provides the clearest hint that Raphael had been called in before Sebastiano). Eighteen months later – on the 2nd July 1518 – Sebastiano himself wrote to Michelangelo saying 'I have delayed, as I did not wish Raphael to see my work before he had delivered his own ... at present I am doing nothing else ... and I think I shall not bring shame on you. Raphael still has not started'.

In the end Raphael did start, but perhaps too late. His contribution – the *Transfiguration* [Fig 3] – may not have been finished at the time of his death in 1520, and it was certainly his pupils who completed it. The *Raising of Lazarus* had been finished by the 1st May 1519 and, although it was successfully exhibited,

Fig 3 Raphael *The Transfiguration* Vatican

the fact that the Cardinal chose to send it to Narbonne and keep Raphael's picture is a sufficient indication of his preference.

Though it is clear from the letters, therefore, that Vasari's account is correct to the extent that Michelangelo was certainly involved in the production of Sebastiano's *Raising of Lazarus* they give no indication of the nature and extent of his participation, so we are thrown back on Vasari's unsupported word. In point of fact he is only slightly more specific. He says that the picture was executed 'in accordance with the arrangement and design in some parts of Michelangelo'. This is generally interpreted to mean that Michelangelo supplied drawings for some of the figures, and this seems indeed to have been the case. It is now usually – though not universally – agreed that two of Michelangelo's preparatory drawings for the *Raising of Lazarus* are now in the British Museum and a third in the Musée Bonnat at Bayonne. These studies [Figs 4, 5, 6] are of great importance as showing the evolution of the picture.

The miracle is described by St. John (11, 33-44) in the following words:- *Jesus therefore again groaning in himself cometh to the grave. It was a cave, and a stone lay upon it. Jesus said, Take ye away the stone. Martha, the sister of him that was dead, saith unto him, Lord, by this time he stinketh: for he hath been dead four days. Jesus saith unto her, Said I not unto thee, that, if thou wouldest believe, thou shouldest see the glory of God? Then they took away the stone from the place where the dead was laid. And Jesus lifted up his eyes, and said, Father, I thank thee that thou hast heard me. And I knew that thou hearest me always: but because of the people which stand by I said it, that they may believe that thou hast sent me. And when he had thus spoken, he cried with a loud voice, Lazarus, come forth. And he that was dead came forth, bound hand and foot with grave clothes: and his face was bound with a napkin. Jesus saith unto them, Loose him, and let him go.*

It is clear from this account that at the sound of Christ's voice Lazarus contrived to raise himself (if he had been buried horizontally) or to come out from the tomb (if he had been vertical) while still bound. In Giotto's fresco of the subject in the

Fig 4 Michelangelo *Study for the Raising of Lazarus* Bayonne, Musée Bonnat

Fig 6 Michelangelo *Study for the Raising of Lazarus* London, The British Museum

Fig 5 Michelangelo *Study for the Raising of Lazarus* London, The British Museum

Fig 7 Giotto *The Raising of Lazarus* Padua, Arena Chapel

Arena Chapel at Padua [Fig 7] Lazarus is erect outside the tomb, but otherwise shows no sign of animation. In the National Gallery picture several episodes are telescoped, but as regards the main figures a slightly later moment is depicted. Some of Lazarus' bands have already been removed from his legs, permitting him to raise one, while he himself is loosening those around his arms and gazing at Christ with an expression of awe.

Fig 8 Michelangelo *Creation of Adam* Vatican, Sistine Chapel

Fig 9 Sebastiano del Piombo *Prophets* Rome, S. Pietro in Montorio

17

This posture seems to have been present in Michelangelo's mind from an early stage, though associated with a different idea. In the Bayonne sheet, which contains two sketches, Lazarus is already seated on the edge of the tomb, and in the British Museum sketches his legs have already assumed the attitude in which they appear in the painting. But in one of them – as in both the Bayonne sketches – there is a significant motive which was finally suppressed. Lazarus stretches out his right hand – evidently to touch the left hand of Christ, as Adam touches the hand of God the Father in Michelangelo's fresco on the Sistine roof [Fig 8]. Lazarus' attitude in this sketch is indeed so reminiscent of Adam's that there can be no doubt that Michelangelo was still thinking along the same lines. But the re-infusion of life into Lazarus did not in fact take place in this way. There was no

Fig 10 Sebastiano del Piombo
Study for the Raising of Lazarus
Frankfurt on Main, Städel Institute

18

contact. Jesus merely called out 'Lazarus, come forth'. And so, in the final British Museum sketch the artist cancelled this idea and retracted Lazarus' right arm, as though undoing the bands. This design also seems to have been used by Sebastiano in the figure of the left-hand prophet in S. Pietro in Montorio [Fig 9].

The earlier of the two British Museum sketches is interesting in another way. At the bottom are four separate studies for a left foot – evidently Christ's. So that although Michelangelo's drawings for this figure have not survived we can deduce that they existed. The British Museum studies leave no doubt that the figures behind Lazarus and underneath him to the spectator's right were also designed by Michelangelo. A sketch for Martha, attributable to Sebastiano himself, now at Frankfurt [Fig 10] shows certain differences from the painting – in her left hand and in the figures in the background – so this figure was probably never of Michelangelo's design.

At this point we may consider briefly an aspect of the affair which seems to have escaped the notice of earlier commentators. We assume that Sebastiano would have received from Michelangelo drawings for the main figures in the *Raising of Lazarus*. These drawings would have adumbrated poses far beyond the power of Sebastiano or anyone else to evolve for himself. But such a situation would itself present a problem of a fiendishly difficult kind – how to devise and fit a large composition round someone else's pre-existing figures. For Michelangelo himself the problem would hardly have arisen – it seems clear from his cartoon of the *Battle of Cascina* that in the case of a multi-figure composition he paid more attention to the single figures than to the whole, and it is a significant confirmation of this interpretation of his working method that he should have chosen this means of 'helping' Sebastiano. But for Sebastiano the problem would have been even more difficult than that which faced Filippino Lippi in the Brancacci chapel of the Carmine at Florence – where he had to complete a large fresco of which Masaccio had painted two detached chunks – and it is right that his astoundingly successful incorporation of Michelangelo's few figures into an harmonious whole should be valued for the feat it represents and due credit for it given.

The fresco of the *Raising of Lazarus* by Giotto, like a similar one by Fra Angelico at S. Marco in Florence, is part of a cycle of scenes from the life of Christ in which this miracle was normally included. They are merely the most famous of many depictions of it in fresco. But as a subject for an altarpiece on a monumental scale it had been very rare indeed, and this distinction is more basic than it might seem. For the functions of frescoes and of altarpieces are not the same. Cycles of frescoes are usually situated on the side walls of a church or chapel. They are meant to be looked at in sequence, and, as it were, read like a book. In consequence, they tend to assume a format which is broader than it is high. But altarpieces, as soon as they evolved into single panels from the earlier Gothic compartments, tended to assume the opposite format. In the case of certain subjects a square or even long shape was sometimes called for. But for architectural reasons the upright format, at least in the case of the main altar, became increasingly usual, while the function of the altarpiece as the focus of attention favoured a theme in which one figure could dominate any others who might be included. Where the subject of the altarpiece was the Madonna and Child this condition was automatically fulfilled, and doubtless for this reason it remained, in one form or another, probably the most common for altarpieces. But during the 15th century there was also an increasing demand for biblical incidents as the subject of altarpieces. Piero della Francesca, Verrocchio, Giovanni Bellini and others painted versions of the Baptism, and in the National Gallery alone there are several other major altarpieces dating from the late 15th century of specific incidents, such as Pollaiuolo's *Martyrdom of S. Sebastian*, Signorelli's *Circumcision* or his *Adoration of the Shepherds*. In consequence, the artist's problem henceforth was to find a method of concentrating into an upright format, with corresponding emphasis on one or two individual figures, incidents which had hitherto been treated expansively.

When, therefore, Sebastiano came to tackle the *Raising of Lazarus* he would have found no real or helpful precedent. We do not know who was responsible for the choice of this subject, but as Raphael's theme, the *Transfiguration*, was also an episode from the life of Christ some measure of co-ordination must have been exercised, and it is therefore unlikely that the choice was entirely that of the artist in either

Fig 11 Raphael *The Procession to Calvary* Madrid, Prado

Fig 12 Ridolfo Ghirlandaio *Procession to Calvary* London, National Gallery

case. Probably it emerged as a result of discussions between the painters and the cardinal's representatives. In Sebastiano's case the lack of precedent was not confined to iconography. In addition there was a stylistic problem. For the new style in which he was working – the so-called High Renaissance style – had still had little or no occasion to produce altarpieces of biblical incidents. Leonardo's only essay in his maturity had been his designs for the Madonna and Child with St. Anne, and Michelangelo, with the exception of the unfinished *Entombment*, of uncertain date, now in the National Gallery, had never tackled an altarpiece at all. Since his arrival in Rome even Raphael had only painted one altarpiece of this kind but it so happened that he had done so just before Sebastiano started working on his, so that it would have been impossible for Sebastiano to ignore it. It represented the Procession to Calvary – the so-called *Spasimo di Sicilia* – executed for Palermo and now in the Prado [Fig 11]. As an engraving of it, by Agostino Veneziano, is dated 1517, the picture must date from then or a little earlier. Its full novelty can most easily be appreciated by comparing it with an earlier example of the same subject, namely the picture painted by Ridolfo Ghirlandaio for the church of S. Gallo and now in the National Gallery [Fig 12].

Ridolfo Ghirlandaio's picture is in fact an altarpiece, but it shirks the problems inherent in the form and could just as easily have been a fresco. The procession moves across the picture space from right to left, as in a relief, and the relief-like quality is echoed by the arrangement of the landscape in the background in a series of parallel planes. Though Christ is in the middle he is not the most conspicuous figure. The one we notice first is the soldier on the left, because of his brightly coloured and elaborately patterned clothes. Much play is also made with subsidiary details, such as the fantastic armour of the horseman and the highly individualised portrait heads. Despite the solemnity of the occasion the result has many of the qualities of a pageant.

Raphael's version of the subject is not pageantry but drama. Instead of Ridolfo Ghirlandaio's even light he shows violent contrasts of light and shade. Instead of moving across our field of vision Christ, who dominates the picture from the centre, almost falls on to us, and the arrangement of the landscape behind assists the effect of movement into and out from the picture. Instead of the timidly-kneeling Veronica Raphael's Virgin Mary makes an impassioned gesture, stretching out both her arms to the fullest extent. No play is made with the details of costume: all are simple and generalised. Above all, there is no suggestion that the occurrence could be paralleled in everyday life. What we are shown is clearly a tremendous event.

Despite Sebastiano's personal antipathy by this time to Raphael – who had earlier been his friend – and despite the help he was receiving from Michelangelo, it seems that Raphael's *Spasimo di Sicilia* was a vital preliminary to the production of Sebastiano's *Raising of Lazarus*. In the latter picture, too, the grand manner is exemplified in the altarpiece of incident. Here, too, the drama is epic, the lighting dramatic, the draperies simplified and the incidental avoided. Again, the figures are highly concentrated within the upright format and fill the whole of the main area with no space showing between them. Again, the characters indulge in noble and varied gestures – the language of dumb-show which Raphael had learnt from Leonardo and which Sebastiano took from him and from Michelangelo. Here again is the deliberately disturbing feature of a figure – in this case Mary Magdalene who kneels in the foreground – gesticulating violently in the direction of the spectator. But, unlike Raphael's picture, the centre of Sebastiano's is calm – the majestic composure of Christ, who advances towards Lazarus with both arms raised.

The transcending of the ordinary in favour of the epic has brought with it a measure of anti-realism in both cases. This is most clearly seen in the perspective. As an altarpiece is raised high above the floor of a church the level of the spectator's eyes is usually below the base of it. Certain painters such as Mantegna had actually painted altarpieces in which this fact is acknowledged. But both Raphael and Sebastiano not only deliberately ignore this fact but also deliberately combine mutually incompatible systems. They both use two separate eye levels within the picture, neither of which is that of the spectator. In the *Raising of Lazarus* we can

Fig 13 Sebastiano del Piombo *Detail from Flagellation* Rome, S. Pietro in Montorio

Fig 14 Sebastiano del Piombo *Detail from Lazarus*

see from the landscape and from the perspective of the stone on which Christ stands, that the eye level of the setting of the picture is very high – almost at the top, as though we were standing with our feet opposite a point half way up the picture. By this means we are able to be shown the landscape, which would be invisible if the scene were shown from the eye level of someone on the floor of the church. But if this high eye level were also applied to the figures they would appear awkwardly foreshortened, with their heads jutting on to their chests and no neck showing. To avoid this they are in fact shown from an eye level at about their waists. The painter in effect has his cake and eats it, and no one is any the worse.

It may seem strange and contradictory that despite the generalised treatment which Sebastiano has extended in some degree to the faces of the figures as well as to their draperies, he has also contrived to introduce a certain measure of portraiture. Yet such seems to be the case, and such, in view of the fact that it was his greatest forte, is hardly surprising. To be convinced of this we need look no farther than the head of the man who appears above Christ's outstretched right arm. His broad face and arresting features must certainly refer to a specific person, and the same applies to most of the other men around Christ. Yet they have not been identified. If it were considered that the use of the features of a living person in a religious picture of this kind did honour to the model, then we should expect to find two men, in particular, commemorated in this way, namely Cardinal Giulio de' Medici, who commissioned the picture, and Michelangelo, who designed part of it. Yet such seems not to be the case. The Cardinal's features as they were recorded at this time by Raphael [Fig 2] do not leap to the eye, nor is there any sign of the unmistakable broken nose of Michelangelo. In point of fact the same features seem to be repeated more than once within the picture, and they also recur in another work by Sebastiano of the same period. The Christ, for instance, is surely the same as the Christ in the *Flagellation* in S. Pietro in Montorio while the scourger on the left in that work [Fig 13] seems to be the same as the Lazarus [Fig 14].

The landscape which Sebastiano has introduced into the top left corner has often been considered a survival of his Venetian practice and an echo of Giorgione. As regards its origin this is probably true. But the scene itself is Roman, and it seems to have inspired so purely Roman a painter as Giulio Romano to incorporate a similar one into his *Stoning of Stephen* [Fig 15], a work which has an important place in the sequence of the High Renaissance altarpiece of incident.

In its completed form the *Raising of Lazarus* is the result of a collaboration of a most unusual kind and of a singular confluence of talent, temperament and opportunity. Inspired by working, as he had already done before, from designs by Michelangelo, and guided, apparently, by Raphael's most recent practice in altarpieces, Sebastiano was able to make his own contribution to the genre and, in the process, to attain to a degree of grandeur and nobility hardly ever achieved before or afterwards. Neither Raphael's *Spasimo di Sicilia* which preceded it, nor Giulio Romano's *Stoning of Stephen* which followed it have an equal sublimity. This is only found, among Renaissance altarpieces, in the *Lazarus*' own rival, Raphael's *Transfiguration*. And even if, as most people would agree, this work is on an even higher plane than the *Raising of Lazarus* it can hardly be doubted that it was the element of rivalry inherent in this singular commission which contributed to making it so.

The later history of the *Lazarus* is less dramatic but by no means uneventful. We do not know the exact date when it reached Narbonne, but it is unlikely to have been long after 1520. It remained there until it was appropriated by the Duc d'Orléans,

Fig 15 Giulio Romano *Martyrdom of S. Stephen* Genoa, S. Stefano

some time before his death in 1723. He was the regent of France during the minority of Louis XV. The dictatorial methods of collecting employed by this bizarre figure are described in a memoir dating from the year of his death:-

'At the same time this prince (the Duc d'Orléans) indulged a different taste. During the coronation at Rheims he had noticed some fine original paintings in the cathedral, and he would not rest until he had them, and had despoiled this church as he had done Narbonne. The Chapter granted him a Titian 14 feet long, a Correggio and other pictures by great masters for which he gave them copies, offering his protection to the Chapter for good measure. He then abandoned his new mistress at Saint-Cloud to come to Paris to see these paintings, and no one could tell which of the two passions was the stronger. The connoisseurs are amazed that he should have a taste for pictures when he clearly has none for arrangement – hanging, as he does, a devotional painting next to a nude, or an architectural piece next to a landscape, to the detriment of both. He only likes amassing in bulk. He told me that when he was in Spain he had permission to have an excellent picture copied in the Escorial, intending to substitute the copy for the original. But the monks got wise to it and had the painter arrested and handed over to the Inquisition.'

In 1771 the *Raising of Lazarus* was transferred, at Paris, from panel to canvas – a revolutionary technique which had been invented some twenty years previously by the French restorer Picault and which has saved many famous pictures from disintegration.

During the French Revolution the *Raising of Lazarus* passed with the rest of the Orléans collection to England, where it was bought, in 1798, by John Julius Angerstein, apparently on the advice of Sir Thomas Lawrence.

After Angerstein bought it, he got the P.R.A., Benjamin West, to restore it – particularly in Lazarus' right leg, above and below the knee. The diarist, Joseph Farington, recorded some of the opinions which were passed on the picture at this

Fig 16 T. Géricault *Raising of Lazarus*
(after Sebastiano) Stuttgart

Fig 17 F. Mackenzie
Interior of No. 100 Pall Mall
London, Victoria and Albert Museum

time. Sir George Beaumont, later a benefactor of the National Gallery, preferred it to the *Transfiguration* of Raphael. Not so the architect, Smirke, or the collector, Sir Francis Bourgeois, who expressed disappointment. The painter, Fuseli, observed that the figure of Lazarus 'showed like one who had been looking into a warm place (Hell) and could hardly believe himself secure from it' while Hazlitt considered that the attendant female figures were 'in a style something between Michelangelo and Parmigianino'.

In 1820-22 the French painter, Théodore Géricault, visited London and painted a smallish sketch copy [Fig 16], now in the Stuttgart gallery, of the *Raising of Lazarus*. In 1824 the vicissitudes of the picture came to an end when it was bought by the Government with the rest of the Angerstein collection to form the nucleus of the National Gallery. For several years it continued to be exhibited in Angerstein's house, No. 100 Pall Mall (since demolished), and it is in this setting that the watercolour by Frederick Mackenzie [Fig 17] shows the *Lazarus* in a place of honour.

Since 1939 the *Raising of Lazarus* has only been exhibited once – for a few weeks, soon after the war. By then the varnish had become so brown that the picture was almost illegible. Subsequently, the disintegration of the ground on which the paint rests and the consequent necessity of renewing it from the back and remounting it on board has involved many years' work. When this was successfully accomplished – and it would take a small book to do justice to the complexity of the work – it was possible to clean the picture and reveal the colours. In effect Lazarus has thus been raised from the dead for the second time.